THE RELAXATION MANIFESTO

by Tim Grimes

For more information visit:

www.radicalcounselor.com

Bulk purchases and speaking

For discounts on bulk purchases, or to invite Tim to speak at your next event, email info@radicalcounselor.com.

ISBN-13: 978-1537638263
ISBN-10: 1537638262

Printed in the United States of America

A personal message from Tim

Don't believe anything I say just at face value. Test it for yourself. If you test it, you'll see if it really works for you – or not. I feel confident that what I'm about to share with you will work, but don't listen to me. Listen to yourself.

THE RELAXATION MANIFESTO

THE LAW OF ATTRACTION can easily overwhelm us. But it doesn't have to.

The intention of this short guide is to eliminate all the stress surrounding the subject. Straightforward advice should make you feel more at ease about how the law of attraction *naturally* functions in your life. Manifesting your desires, in my opinion, should be fun and easy, and never too stressful. Anxiety doesn't need to be there. And if it's not there, the law of attraction will start working for you.

Let me tell you a personal anecdote to begin illustrating this point. When I became interested in the law of attraction, I read a lot of advice on the topic. Nonetheless, like many others, I struggled to apply it to my own life. I gradually became anxious about the manifesting process. Certain things that I hoped would manifest quickly, such as more money, failed to materialize. Even though I'd received good recommendations, I began thinking it was hard to actually make the law of attraction work.

Many of you probably have had similar concerns. However, what was interesting about my situation was that I was *wrong* about the law of attraction not initially working. I know now that the "failures" I had at the beginning of my manifesting journey weren't failures at all. For instance, while I didn't get more money when I began applying manifestation principles, I did suddenly have more free time on my hands. This welcome shift in my schedule was subtle, and I only fully noticed it in retrospect. I didn't see it as a result of the law of attraction while it was happening. But, it *was* the result of that.

More free time was what I really felt I needed at that period of my life. And it suddenly appeared. I never applied serious effort trying to manifest more free time – but I naturally *felt it* when I did my manifesting exercises, so it quickly showed up anyway. Meanwhile, piles of abstract money didn't feel real to me, even though I constantly did manifesting exercises with them in mind, and they didn't show up.

This is a good example of how understated the law of attraction usually is. While I actively thought about money while performing manifesting exercises, what I actually strongly *felt* was an increased amount of free time. The money didn't come to me because I was only *thinking* about it – often anxiously – while more time to do what I wanted did come because I felt it as being real. The entire process happened in such a subdued manner I hardly noticed it, and illustrates a point you've probably heard many times before, but is worth repeating here…

Manifestation is about feeling, not thinking.

The law of attraction is rarely as dramatic as we expect. It's essentially a practical concept, when we get down to its core. It's not your individual thoughts that matter; it's the deepest feelings those thoughts elicit that count. And if you investigate this concept further, you realize that if you draw out positive feelings within yourself – if you simply focus on *feeling good* – then you cannot fail in having good things happen to you.

This is a fundamental part of the law of attraction. If we cultivate relaxed, gratifying feelings associated with already having something we want, then we *already feel* we have it in that moment. We psychologically have it now. We believe we actually have it. It's not coming. It's already *here*. You *have* it. You *feel* it. That feeling is real.

This deep inner feeling of something being real will also eventually become real in our outer world – even though right now it's "just" a feeling – if we don't subsequently destroy the feeling by pushing it away. If we start feeling something as being real with consistency, sooner or later, that feeling will begin expressing itself in our physical world. This is another fundamental feature of the law of attraction.

Feeling something as being real is triggered by relaxation. Relaxation allows you to easily utilize the law of attraction, and alters your relationship with the concept. So the premise of this guide is that we don't need to *try hard* to get what we want. We can *relax* instead.

In my opinion, the law of attraction is usually more about stress reduction than anything else. Manifesting is the practice of reducing stress and feeling more relaxed throughout our everyday routine. It's *not* about being some perfectly peaceful yogi up on a hill, or anything particularly spiritual. It's not magical – it's practical. You want a simple method to receive more good things in your life? *Feel more relaxed!* That's it.

But it's easier said than done. And the reason for that is because we have no idea how to relax with any type of consistency. Feeling relaxed, ironically, is difficult. Most of us are habitual worriers. We get confused about relaxation, because we've inadvertently been taught how to strive, worry, and try hard – not how to relax.

We don't need to strive, or try, to be relaxed. Relaxation is the opposite of trying hard and using willpower. It's a *lack* of serious mental effort. You already know what it means to be relaxed, and you've experienced it countless times before in your life. You like it. It gives you a sense of inner peace. It doesn't involve overthinking, worrying, or overanalyzing. You feel good when you're relaxed, and it feels right. There's a sense of effortlessness about the whole thing. No one has to tell you when you're relaxed – *you know.*

But, unfortunately, you probably don't feel relaxed as much as you'd like.

A practical way to help solve this problem is to integrate feelings of relaxation into more parts of your life – start making it habitual – instead of cultivating the rational problem-solving type of thinking that we're so inclined to use. We've accidently been taught to value being anxious by always *thinking* of solutions, and this proves to be counterproductive.

Overthinking doesn't solve problems; it causes problems.

When we have to think rationally about something, we should. Clearly there's nothing wrong with this. But if you observe your thoughts throughout the day, you'll probably notice that's not what you're doing. Your rational thinking is running haywire most of the time. It's not solving problems; it's usually *creating* them. While it's fine to think rationally, most of us are doing it way more than we want. And this overly-active thinking hinders our ability to be relaxed and enjoy ourselves. If you pay attention to your thoughts and emotions, you'll notice this. It may surprise you, but you'll likely come to realize that you're more mentally high-strung than you believed.

Instead of worrying about things, we should allow ourselves an alternative option. However, just because it sounds nice to be more relaxed doesn't mean we'll actually *do it*. And this is why it's a practice – even though it seems funny to label relaxation as a practice.

Believe me, it's a practice.

You have to acknowledge how anxious your thoughts often are – and probably have been for a long time – and then gently work with them. This takes some patience and maturity. The good news is that you'll *want* to work on this, because it's a win-win situation. You'll want to feel relaxed – because you like feeling relaxed – and it'll also make other aspects of your life significantly better.

So, let me emphasize something obvious: To facilitate relaxation, it helps to do activities you find relaxing. Many of us feel guilty if we relax too much – which is ridiculous. We don't need to feel guilty about anything, let alone relaxing.

It's smart to relax more, rather than less.

The choice of what you do to help you relax is yours. Here are a few common and uncommon examples to make you start considering the numerous stress reduction options available: taking a walk, yoga, deep breathing exercises, self-hypnosis, drinking a few glasses of wine, making love, flying a kite, building a bookshelf, lying in bed, golfing, singing out loud, riding a dirt bike, folding laundry, spinning in circles, drawing, swimming, eating chocolate, playing tennis, water skiing, sitting in a steam room, listening to soothing music, playing checkers, sipping scotch, eating a good meal, sunbathing, dancing, watching a TV series, cooking, getting a pedicure, reading a detective novel...

The list goes on and on. It's your call as to what makes you relaxed, no one else's. Think out of the box with it, and don't worry if the activities that calm you down seem mundane or unorthodox. Such activities are great as long as they work. It's not difficult to quickly reduce stress and feel more relaxed if you make up your mind to do it (if you're confused about this, refer to my guide *Wild Calm* and the supplemental material at the end of this guide.)

If we start putting an emphasis on stress reduction, good things happen. Our habitual tension will begin to unravel somewhat, and we'll start feeling better. Again, this is practical advice, and it doesn't need to be rushed or forced. We like to feel relaxed, and what I'm telling you is, if you actually *do* this – if you practice stress reduction and becoming more relaxed – then positive things will happen to you without any other manifesting activities being done on your part.

The law of attraction often works best when you don't even think about it. Being relaxed, instead of stressed, enables that to happen. There's never any pressure. Pressure is the opposite of relaxation; pressure is a byproduct of thinking too much. Allow yourself, if you feel like it, to relax instead.

When you're relaxed, you don't need to think of anything special or complicated, unless you want to. You can just relax, and go about doing whatever you're doing. Be your normal self. Let relaxation become more of your mental default option as you move throughout your day. Subtle anxiety is usually our mental default option, and this is a nicer alternative.

Relaxation is almost always the underrated key to the law of attraction process. Yes, there are numerous law of attraction "tricks" we hear about that can make things show up in our lives quickly. But those tricks don't usually *work*...unless we already feel relaxed. Being relaxed about things is different than trying hard to manifest something, and it *feels* much easier. It's such a relief just to be able to do that and go with the flow. A burden is lifted, which changes things.

Don't think excessively about what you have to do to make something happen. Relax instead.

Now, when you begin practicing this, there will be plenty of times when you'll *not* feel relaxed at all. Perfect. Good – that means you're aware you're not relaxed. We have a lot of habitual tension, which is fine, and it unsurprisingly shows up in our physical feelings and thoughts.

So failing to feel relaxed is to be expected.

Don't be shocked if you can't relax with any type of consistency. Don't be afraid if your anxious thoughts run wild. You can smile to yourself and acknowledge it. No big deal. There's nothing wrong with you – that's normal.

Please don't ever strive for perfection while practicing being more relaxed.

That'd be a terrible mistake. *Never* strive for perfection. Actually, if you can, I'd suggest never striving at all. Period. Get over yourself. Be normal, not special. If you're stressed – fine. Good. Excellent. No problem. Sometimes you're going to feel scared, angry, embarrassed, nervous, sad, pissed off, jealous or worried. Those are normal emotions. You should probably expect them to be there. You should expect to still feel weird and uncomfortable sometimes. Don't suppress those emotions. There's nothing wrong with *any* of them. Trying to mentally force them away will usually prove to be counterproductive.

And, nonetheless, amidst all those bumpy emotions...just gently *get back* to feeling relaxed.

Take your time. Gradually, come back to your new emotional emphasis – which is feeling relaxed. Those "uncomfortable" emotions won't stick around forever, and you'll want to come back to a relaxed center point, because it feels good, and it will *naturally* happen if you lightly focus on it.

You don't have to force it back – and don't worry if it doesn't happen right away. We worry enough already, so you don't have to worry about not being relaxed enough. If we find ourselves feeling like crap, we might as well be relaxed about the whole thing. What else are we going to do that's *actually* emotionally productive in such a situation? Why be so serious about it? Trying hard to dig ourselves out of an emotional hole usually works poorly. It's better to laugh about it if we can.

Over time, by practicing being more relaxed, the inner tension you feel inside yourself will begin to shift. This probably *will not* be a transformative experience, and it doesn't need to be. But you'll start being able to unwind more easily and consistently. Be patient with your thoughts and how your body physically feels. Don't rush anything. If you still often find yourself getting nervous, upset, or angry, that's fine and normal. Don't expect your emotions to magically change overnight or within a few months. Why would they? They don't need to. Take it easy. Don't worry about stuff like that.

Just relax.

Your body *knows* how it wants to feel moment from moment. Practicing being relaxed will help you realize this. We often hold ourselves up to impossibly high standards – hoping to mimic so-called "enlightened teachers" that we've never intimately known – and this makes it so we have no choice but to self-sabotage ourselves. We refuse to admit that it's perfectly fine to be a normal human being. We create an unnecessary cycle of self-inflicted pain because we're not okay with being who we are. Don't allow yourself to get caught up in this cycle of self-judgment. Don't try to emulate or idolize anyone else.

Stop judging yourself, stop being serious, and just relax instead.

None of this is difficult if we stop constantly judging ourselves. Personally, if this was difficult, I wouldn't be doing it. Most of the time, if something isn't easy, it isn't worth doing. I learned that the hard way, and I'm sure many of you have too. So don't worry about this being hard. It's not hard. It's just *different*. It's a totally different paradigm than what we're used to, and it takes time getting used to this new paradigm. But the whole thing should be effective and simple.

Just relax.

That's it. When we feel relaxed, things flow more smoothly. Is there anything specific we should think about when we're relaxed? Not really, unless we *want* to be thinking about something. It's fine to think about things we desire when we're relaxed. But you don't have to think about *anything* if you don't want to. Just be relaxed, and go about your life. That's all you have to do. This isn't esoteric. Gently allow yourself to:

1. *Go within.*
2. *Get relaxed.*
3. *Stay relaxed.*

That's an exercise worth doing with consistency, and it's much healthier than getting on a treadmill. Granted, I *know* it's much easier to say it than to actually *do* it – but still, just do it.

Who cares if you have problems with this exercise? Get back to doing it when you're ready again. Simple autosuggestion is one thing that can help make it easier. For instance, you can repeat soothing words like *"tranquil, calm, peace"* to yourself for a few minutes when you wake up and before going to sleep at night. If you repeat words like those with faith and conviction each day, you'll inevitably deepen your sense of relaxation (see the supplemental material at the end of this guide for more information on autosuggestion.)

You'll want to get back to feeling relaxed, and you'll get better at it with practice. Get relaxed and stay relaxed. I mean, is there any *real* good reason not to be relaxed?

Frankly…no.

Don't take my word for it, though. Talk is very, very cheap. *Test it*. Our thoughts might work against us when we feel agitated, but our thoughts *will work for us* once we feel relaxed. Intuitively, you'll know this when it's happening. You already know it, because you've experienced it before in your life. Something just feels right. It feels right because *it is* right. We become aligned with a peaceful and productive state simply by being relaxed. This is worth acknowledging, because people usually hear about the law of attraction and get overly excited about *trying* to get it to work for them.

Please don't try.

The law of attraction doesn't work like that. Life doesn't work like that. The way life usually works well for us is when we're relaxed, whether we're aware of it or not. So don't try. Don't worry. Don't think. Don't listen to me. Just relax.

Not many of us will allow ourselves this luxury. Most of us have no idea what *actually* happens when we do it. It's a potentially life-altering thing. But it's so subtle and non-dramatic we hardly pay it any mind. We don't meet adults who say life is too easy, even though our lives often *are* easy. We just don't notice it, because we tend to focus on the negative stuff; we tend to worry. And so no one ever complains about how easy life is. It's always too hard, never too easy. What a lousy paradigm to follow. Yet that's basically what we all do!

Do you really want to follow the brilliant advice of people who are always quietly complaining about how hard their life is? Well, most of us do, even if we're not directly aware of it. This positive information about relaxation is unfortunately never taught to us.

We have no idea that life doesn't have to be continually crappy, just because the majority of adults imply it's crappy by what they say and how they act.

Now you know more about the deeper benefits of relaxation. So just relax. When in doubt, always relax. There's nothing to do, nothing that needs to be done. If you get into this, you'll realize there's really nothing you *can* do. Free will, as most of us think of it, *doesn't* actually exist. And this realization in itself provides a huge relief. The belief that you always need to do something dissipates when you realize it's a lie.

Life just happens, whether we like it or not. So we might as well relax, if we can. In this way, things can be manifested even if we have no familiarity with the law of attraction. Our family life, for instance, might unexpectedly improve, or our health might surprisingly get better. These occurrences, to an outsider unaware of your inner actions, will appear to be a coincidence, and they might even seem to be a coincidence to you. They're not. They're because you're more consistently relaxed. You're finally allowing yourself to give into life by relaxing more. You might be stunned with how friendly life begins treating you in return.

Supplemental Information

Again, I advise you to test everything in this guide, and not to just blindly believe me. Don't trust me; trust the results you get. Relax and know you're your own best teacher. Below are a few additional recommendations – or "tricks" – that I think you'll enjoy:

- Stop being so serious!

You'll probably be shocked with what happens when you become completely playful for just a minute or two. Do you really suffer, except when you take your thinking so seriously? Find out by momentarily becoming entirely playful.

I have free video tutorials showing you easy ways to be less serious over at *www.stopbeingserious.com*. You can also refer to my written guide *Wild Calm*. By being less serious, we can quickly reduce stress and relax into the present moment. This is simple information anyone can utilize.

- Practice autosuggestion.

This is another tool that's so simple that most people overlook it in favor of more complicated and less effective recommenda-tions. Just by repeating a word or phrase with faith for a short time each day – such as *"happy," "healthy," "free,"* or similar words/phrases that resonate with you – you can change your life.

Autosuggestion sounds too good to be true. It's not. Émile Coué was one of the great teachers of the 20th century, and I highly recommend his method, which is startling in its clarity. You can repeat a single word, a string of positive words, or a simple powerful phrase such as Coué's *"Day by day, in every way, I'm getting better and better."*

Extensive information on Coué's auto-suggestion method can be found online.

Other guides from Tim include:

WILD CALM
A Direct Approach to Happiness

RELAX MORE, TRY LESS
The Easy Path to Abundance

MINDFUL MANIFESTATION
A Uniquely Effective Way to Practice Mindfulness

MANIFESTATION THROUGH RELAXATION
A Guide to Getting More by Giving In

The Relaxation Manifesto

Keynote or Workshop

Tim Grimes *speaks authoritatively on topics centered around stress relief, work-life balance and personal fulfillment. Based upon his unique background and experience, Tim shares surprising ways for everyone to become more productive and fulfilled by embracing relaxation as a paradigm for success.*

To invite Tim to speak at your next event, email:

info@radicalcounselor.com

For more information visit:

www.radicalcounselor.com

Printed in Great Britain
by Amazon